Relationships

Unlock the Secrets to Lasting Love, Fulfilling Connections, and Happy Relationships: A Guide to Transforming Your Personal and Professional Interactions

Lance P. Richards

Relationships: Unlock the Secrets to Lasting Love, Fulfilling Connections, and Happy Relationships: A Guide to Transforming Your Personal and Professional Interactions

Table of Contents

01: Introduction: The Power of Positive Relationships

Relationships are a fundamental aspect of our lives, shaping who we are and how we interact with the world around us. From the relationships we have with our family and friends, to those we develop in the workplace, they have the power to bring us joy, fulfillment, and happiness, but they can also be the source of pain, conflict, and disappointment. In order to build strong, lasting relationships, it is essential to understand the secrets that unlock the full potential of these connections.

At the heart of positive relationships is the concept of positive communication. Effective communication is the key to building trust, resolving conflicts, and fostering emotional intimacy. Positive communication requires active listening, empathy, and the ability to understand and respond to the needs and feelings of others. It also involves setting healthy boundaries and respecting the boundaries of others, as well as being able to apologize and forgive when needed.

Emotional intelligence is another critical component of positive relationships. It involves being able to understand, manage, and express our own emotions, as well as being able to understand and respond to the emotions of others. A high level of emotional intelligence allows us to navigate the ups and downs of relationships with greater ease and to build stronger connections with those around us.

The impact of technology on relationships cannot be overstated. The rapid pace of technological change has transformed the way we communicate, interact, and form relationships. While technology has made it easier to connect with others, it has also created new challenges, including the need to navigate digital relationships, manage the boundaries between online and offline relationships, and minimize the negative impact of technology on our mental health and well-being.

In this guide, we will explore the secrets to lasting love, fulfilling connections, and happy relationships. We will examine the key elements of positive relationships, including communication, emotional intelligence, and the impact of technology, and provide practical tips and strategies for building and maintaining strong, positive relationships. Whether you are seeking to improve your love life, enhance your professional connections, or build stronger relationships with friends and family, this guide will provide you with the tools and insights you need to transform your relationships and unlock the full potential of your connections. So let's get started on this journey towards a brighter and more fulfilling future!

02: Understanding Yourself: The Key to Effective Communication

Before we can truly connect with others in meaningful and fulfilling relationships, it is essential to have a deep understanding of ourselves. This means recognizing our own emotions, motivations, and values, as well as knowing our strengths and weaknesses. By gaining a deeper understanding of who we are and what is important to us, we are better equipped to communicate effectively with others and build stronger relationships.

Effective communication is a critical component of positive relationships. It involves being able to express our thoughts, feelings, and needs in a clear, concise, and non-threatening way, while also being able to actively listen to and understand the perspectives and feelings of others. To achieve effective communication, it is essential to have self-awareness, emotional intelligence, and an understanding of our own communication styles.

Self-awareness is the ability to understand and recognize our own thoughts, feelings, and behaviors. This means being able to identify our own emotions and understand how they impact our interactions with others. By developing

self-awareness, we can better understand our own motivations and triggers, and respond to challenges and conflicts
in a more constructive and effective manner.

Emotional intelligence involves the ability to understand,
manage, and express our own emotions, as well as being
able to understand and respond to the emotions of others.
This requires being able to identify our own emotions and
recognize how they impact our interactions with others, as
well as being able to manage our emotional reactions in a
way that promotes positive relationships. A high level of
emotional intelligence also involves being able to communicate effectively with others and build strong, positive relationships.

Our communication styles also play a key role in our ability
to connect with others. Some people are more direct and
straightforward in their communication, while others are
more indirect and use humor or sarcasm to express themselves. Understanding our own communication style, as
well as the communication styles of others, is critical for
building effective relationships. By recognizing the different
communication styles of those around us, we can adapt our

own style to better connect with others and build stronger relationships.

In this chapter, we will explore the key elements of self-awareness, emotional intelligence, and communication styles, and provide practical tips and strategies for improving our ability to understand ourselves and communicate effectively with others. By gaining a deeper understanding of ourselves and our communication styles, we can build stronger relationships, reduce conflict, and improve our overall happiness and well-being. So let's dive in and start building the foundation for a lifetime of positive relationships!

03: Building Trust: The Foundation of Strong Relationships

Trust is the foundation of all strong relationships, whether they are personal or professional. It is the glue that holds relationships together and provides the basis for mutual respect, cooperation, and understanding. Without trust, relationships can become strained and even break down, causing pain and disappointment for all involved. Building trust is therefore a critical component of creating positive and fulfilling relationships.

So what is trust and how is it built? Trust is a belief in the reliability, truth, or ability of someone or something. In relationships, trust is built by demonstrating reliability, consistency, and dependability over time. This means following through on commitments, being honest and transparent, and treating others with respect and kindness. Trust is also built through shared experiences and the ability to confide in one another.

Effective communication is also critical to building trust in relationships. When we communicate openly and honestly, we build a foundation of trust that allows us to better understand one another and work through conflicts and challenges. Positive communication involves active listening, empathy, and the ability to express our thoughts and feelings in a clear and non-threatening way. By improving our communication skills, we can build stronger relationships and lay the foundation for a lifetime of trust and mutual understanding.

Building trust also requires a high level of emotional intelligence. When we are able to understand and manage our own emotions, as well as recognize and respond to the emotions of others, we create a safe and supportive environment that promotes trust and fosters positive relationships. A high level of emotional intelligence also involves being able to communicate effectively with others and build strong, positive relationships.

The impact of technology on relationships can also have a significant impact on trust. In the digital age, it can be difficult to know who to trust and when to trust them. However, by using technology in a responsible and respectful manner, we can build trust and create positive relationships online. This means being mindful of privacy and security, avoiding online gossip and negativity, and being mindful of the impact of technology on our mental health and well-being.

In this chapter, we will explore the key elements of building trust, including communication, emotional intelligence, and the impact of technology, and provide practical tips and strategies for creating and maintaining strong, trusting relationships. By following these principles, we can build strong, positive relationships that are based on trust, respect, and mutual understanding. So let's start building the foundation for a lifetime of fulfilling relationships!

04: Setting Healthy Boundaries: Maintaining Your Identity in Relationships

Boundaries are an essential part of healthy relationships. They define who we are and what we are willing to accept from others. By setting and maintaining healthy boundaries, we protect our physical, emotional, and mental well-being, and we ensure that our relationships are based on mutual respect, trust, and understanding.

However, setting and maintaining healthy boundaries can be challenging, especially in relationships where one person may try to dominate or control the other. In these situations, it is important to stand up for yourself and assert your boundaries, even if it means facing conflict or discomfort. By setting and maintaining healthy boundaries, you are communicating to others what is acceptable behavior, and you are protecting your own well-being and independence.

To set healthy boundaries, it is important to start by understanding your own values and beliefs. What do you consider to be non-negotiable in a relationship? What are your personal and emotional needs? Understanding these things will help you to communicate your boundaries effectively to others.

Next, it is important to communicate your boundaries clearly and directly. This means expressing your needs and expectations in a calm and assertive manner, and being willing to listen to the needs and concerns of others. If conflicts arise, it is important to seek resolution in a non-violent and non-judgmental manner.

In addition to setting boundaries, it is also important to maintain your own identity and individuality within relationships. This means not losing yourself or compromising your values or beliefs, and being true to who you are. By maintaining your own identity, you are better able to establish healthy relationships based on mutual respect and understanding.

It is also important to understand that boundaries can and should change over time. As relationships grow and evolve, our needs and expectations may change, and it is important to reassess and adjust our boundaries accordingly. By doing so, we can ensure that our relationships remain healthy, positive, and fulfilling.

04: SETTING HEALTHY BOUNDARIES: MAINTAINING YOUR IDENTITY IN RELATIONSHIPS

Finally, it is important to recognize that not all relationships are healthy or positive, and in some cases, it may be necessary to end a relationship in order to protect your well-being and maintain your boundaries. When this occurs, it is important to do so in a respectful and dignified manner, and to seek support from family and friends as needed.

In this chapter, we will explore the key elements of setting and maintaining healthy boundaries in relationships, and provide practical tips and strategies for creating positive and fulfilling relationships that are based on mutual respect, trust, and understanding. By following these principles, we can ensure that our relationships are healthy, positive, and fulfilling, and that we are able to maintain our own identity and well-being.

05: Emotional Intelligence: Navigating Emotions in Relationships

Emotional intelligence is the ability to understand and manage our own emotions, as well as the emotions of others. It is a key factor in building and maintaining healthy relationships, both personal and professional. By developing our emotional intelligence, we are better able to navigate the complex emotions that arise in relationships, and we are better equipped to build strong and fulfilling connections with others.

One of the key components of emotional intelligence is self-awareness. This means being aware of our own emotions and how they impact our thoughts and behaviors. By becoming more self-aware, we are better able to regulate our emotions, and we are less likely to react impulsively or in harmful ways.

Another important component of emotional intelligence is empathy, or the ability to understand and share the feelings of others. This means being able to put ourselves in another person's shoes, and to understand their perspective and emotional state. By developing our empathy, we are better able to connect with others, to build trust and understanding, and to resolve conflicts in a positive and constructive manner.

In addition to self-awareness and empathy, emotional intelligence also involves the ability to regulate our own emotions, and to respond to others in a calm and rational manner, even in challenging situations. This means managing our own stress levels, and avoiding knee-jerk reactions that can escalate conflicts and damage relationships.

Another important aspect of emotional intelligence is the ability to communicate effectively. This means expressing our needs and feelings in a clear and assertive manner, and being willing to listen to the needs and feelings of others. By developing our communication skills, we are better able to build trust and understanding, and to navigate the emotional complexities of relationships.

In relationships, it is also important to recognize that emotions can run high, and that conflicts are an inevitable part of any relationship. When conflicts do arise, it is important to approach them in a calm and rational manner, and to seek resolution in a non-violent and non-judgmental way. By doing so, we can avoid damaging our relationships, and we can build stronger and more resilient connections with others.

In this chapter, we will explore the key elements of emotional intelligence, and provide practical tips and strategies for developing your emotional intelligence and navigating the emotions that arise in relationships. By following these principles, we can build stronger and more fulfilling relationships, and we can create positive and supportive connections with others that last a lifetime.

06: Active Listening: A Critical Skill for Connecting with Others

Active listening is a key skill for building strong and fulfilling relationships, both personal and professional. It involves fully paying attention to what the other person is saying, both verbally and non-verbally, and demonstrating that you understand and value their thoughts and feelings. When done effectively, active listening can help build trust, deepen understanding, and resolve conflicts in a positive and constructive manner.

There are several key elements of active listening, including paying attention, withholding judgment, asking clarifying questions, and providing feedback. When we pay attention, we are fully present in the moment, and we are focused on what the other person is saying. We avoid distractions, such as checking our phones or daydreaming, and we give the other person our full attention.

Withholding judgment is another important aspect of active listening. This means avoiding the urge to interrupt, dismiss, or dismiss the other person's thoughts and feelings. By withholding judgment, we demonstrate respect for the other person, and we create a safe and supportive environment for open and honest communication.

Asking clarifying questions is another important aspect of active listening. This means asking questions to better understand the other person's perspective, and to gain a deeper understanding of their thoughts and feelings. By asking clarifying questions, we demonstrate that we are truly listening, and we show the other person that their thoughts and feelings are valued.

Finally, providing feedback is an important aspect of active listening. This means offering verbal and non-verbal responses that demonstrate that we understand and value the other person's thoughts and feelings. Feedback can be as simple as nodding in agreement, or making eye contact, or as complex as summarizing the other person's perspective and offering support.

In relationships, active listening is a powerful tool for building trust, resolving conflicts, and deepening understanding. When we actively listen to our partners, friends, and colleagues, we demonstrate that we value their perspectives, and we create a safe and supportive environment for open and honest communication.

06: ACTIVE LISTENING: A CRITICAL SKILL FOR CONNECTING WITH OTHERS

However, active listening can be challenging, especially in situations where emotions run high, or where there are underlying differences or conflicts. In these situations, it is important to stay calm, to withhold judgment, and to approach the conversation in a positive and constructive manner. By doing so, we can effectively navigate the challenges of relationships, and we can build stronger and more fulfilling connections with others.

In this chapter, we will explore the key elements of active listening, and provide practical tips and strategies for improving your active listening skills. By following these principles, we can build stronger and more fulfilling relationships, and we can create positive and supportive connections with others that last a lifetime.

07: Resolving Conflict: Strategies for Overcoming Differences

Conflict is a natural and inevitable part of all relationships, whether they are personal or professional. It can arise from differences in opinion, values, goals, or interests, and it can be triggered by misunderstandings, miscommunications, or unmet needs. While conflict can be challenging, it can also provide an opportunity for growth, learning, and relationship strengthening.

To effectively resolve conflicts in relationships, it is important to approach them in a positive and constructive manner. This means avoiding blame, criticism, or attack, and instead focusing on finding a mutually beneficial solution. By doing so, we can overcome differences and build stronger and more fulfilling relationships.

There are several key strategies for resolving conflict in relationships, including:

– Identifying and Understanding the Issue: The first step in resolving conflict is to identify and understand what is at the root of the issue. This means looking beyond the symptoms and instead focusing on the underlying cause.

07: RESOLVING CONFLICT: STRATEGIES FOR OVER-COMING DIFFERENCES

— Effective Communication: Communication is key to resolving conflict. It is important to listen actively and openly to the other person's perspective, and to express your own thoughts and feelings in a clear and respectful manner.

— Seeking Common Ground: When resolving conflict, it is important to seek common ground, and to find areas of agreement. By doing so, you can build a shared understanding and establish a foundation for resolving the conflict.

— Emphasizing the Positive: Instead of focusing on what is wrong, it is important to emphasize the positive and to find ways to build on what is working in the relationship. By doing so, you can shift the conversation from a negative to a positive direction.

— Negotiating a Solution: To resolve conflict, it is important to negotiate a solution that is mutually beneficial. This may involve compromising, or finding a solution that addresses everyone's needs and interests.

— Building Trust: Trust is a critical component of all relationships, and it is particularly important when resolving conflict. By building trust, you can create a safe and supportive environment for open and honest communication, which can help resolve conflicts in a positive and constructive manner.

In this chapter, we will explore these strategies in more detail, and provide practical tips and guidance for effectively resolving conflicts in relationships. By following these principles, you can overcome differences, build stronger and more fulfilling relationships, and create positive and supportive connections with others that last a lifetime.

08: The Art of Apology: Repairing Damaged Relationships

Apology is an important tool for repairing damaged relationships, and for restoring trust, connection, and understanding between people. An apology is a formal expression of regret or remorse for having caused harm or offense to someone, and it can be a powerful way to heal the emotional wounds of conflict and rebuild relationships.

However, apologies are not always easy to make, and many people struggle with the process. This can be due to feelings of shame, guilt, or embarrassment, or to a lack of understanding about what constitutes a genuine and effective apology.

To make a meaningful and effective apology, there are several key elements to consider, including:

– Accepting Responsibility: The first step in making an apology is to accept responsibility for your actions. This means acknowledging the harm or offense that you have caused, and taking ownership of your behavior.

– Expressing Regret: An apology should always include an

expression of regret, remorse, or sorrow. This can be done by saying "I am sorry" or "I regret that I caused this harm".

– Making Amends: Making amends is a critical component of an apology. This may involve repairing the damage that was done, compensating the person for any losses, or taking steps to prevent the same thing from happening again in the future.

– Seeking Forgiveness: Apologizing is about seeking forgiveness, not about expecting it. When making an apology, it is important to acknowledge that you cannot control the other person's response, and to respect their decision to forgive or not forgive.

– Learning from the Experience: Finally, an apology should be an opportunity to learn from the experience, and to make changes in your behavior to prevent similar conflicts from occurring in the future.

In this chapter, we will explore these elements of an effective apology, and provide guidance for making apologies that are sincere, meaningful, and effective. We will also look at how to repair damaged relationships, and how to use apolo-

gies as a tool for growth, learning, and personal transforma-
tion.

By understanding the power of apology, and by putting its
principles into practice, you can build stronger and more
fulfilling relationships, and unlock the secrets to lasting
love, fulfilling connections, and happy relationships.

09: Forgiveness: Moving Forward from Past Hurt

Forgiveness is a powerful tool for healing past hurt and for restoring relationships that have been damaged by conflict, disappointment, or betrayal. Forgiveness allows us to let go of negative feelings and resentments, and to move forward in a positive and constructive way. It can also help us to release feelings of anger, hurt, or pain, and to find peace and resolution in the aftermath of difficult experiences.

However, forgiveness can be a challenging and complex process, and it often requires us to work through a range of difficult emotions and experiences. This can include facing the reality of the harm that was done, acknowledging our own pain and vulnerability, and taking steps to rebuild trust and connection.

To effectively forgive someone, there are several key elements to consider, including:

– Acknowledging Your Own Emotions: Before you can forgive someone, it is important to acknowledge your own emotions and feelings about the situation. This includes recognizing the pain and hurt that you have experienced, as well as any anger or resentment that you may be feeling.

– Understanding the Other Person's Perspective: To effectively forgive someone, it is also important to understand their perspective and motivations. This may involve seeking to understand their experiences, feelings, and circumstances that led to their actions.

– Letting Go of Resentment: Forgiveness requires letting go of resentment, anger, and negative feelings, and choosing instead to focus on positive and constructive outcomes. This can be a challenging process, and may involve working through feelings of hurt and betrayal, and learning to trust again.

– Moving Forward: Forgiveness is not just about letting go of the past, but also about moving forward in a positive and constructive way. This may involve taking steps to rebuild the relationship, or to establish new patterns of behavior that promote healing and growth.

In this chapter, we will explore these elements of forgiveness, and provide guidance for how to effectively forgive others and to move forward from past hurt. We will also look at how to support and encourage others to forgive, and how to build relationships based on trust, understanding, and mutual respect.

By understanding the power of forgiveness, and by putting its principles into practice, you can transform past hurt into opportunities for growth and learning, and create lasting and fulfilling relationships that are based on love, connection, and happiness.

10: Communication in Relationships: Overcoming Barriers and Improving Connection

Introduction

Effective communication is a crucial component of any healthy relationship, whether it be a romantic partnership, a friendship, or a professional collaboration. It is through communication that we build trust, express our needs and desires, and resolve conflicts. Unfortunately, communication can also be one of the greatest barriers to a fulfilling relationship. Misunderstandings, miscommunication, and unspoken expectations can all lead to hurt feelings, misunderstandings, and even the breakdown of a relationship.

Overcoming Barriers to Communication

One of the biggest challenges in communication is overcoming the barriers that prevent us from effectively connecting with others. Some of these barriers include:

– Filters: Our own personal filters, such as past experiences, beliefs, and emotions, can cloud our ability to clearly understand what others are saying and vice versa.

10: COMMUNICATION IN RELATIONSHIPS: OVERCOMING BARRIERS AND IMPROVING CONNECTION

– Emotional barriers: Emotional barriers can prevent us from effectively communicating our thoughts and feelings, leading to misunderstandings and misinterpretations.

– Language barriers: Even if we speak the same language, misunderstandings can still occur due to differences in regional dialects, accents, or cultural differences.

– Technology barriers: With the increasing use of technology in our daily lives, it can be tempting to rely on digital communication instead of face-to-face interactions. However, this can lead to misunderstandings and miscommunication due to the lack of nonverbal cues.

Strategies for Improving Communication

Fortunately, there are several strategies that we can use to overcome these barriers and improve our communication in relationships:

– Practice active listening: Active listening involves fully focusing on what the other person is saying and acknowledging their perspective. This can help to build trust and understanding, and prevent misunderstandings.

10: COMMUNICATION IN RELATIONSHIPS: OVERCOM-
ING BARRIERS AND IMPROVING CONNECTION

– Use "I" statements: Instead of blaming or accusing others, use "I" statements to express your thoughts and feelings. This can help to avoid defensiveness and encourage open communication.

– Avoid assumptions: Assuming that we know what others are thinking or feeling can lead to misunderstandings. Instead, ask questions and clarify to avoid assumptions.

– Be mindful of nonverbal cues: Nonverbal cues such as body language, tone of voice, and facial expressions can often convey more than words alone. Paying attention to these cues can help to improve understanding and avoid miscommunication.

– Take time to reflect: After a conversation, take some time to reflect on what was said and how you felt. This can help to identify areas for improvement and prevent future misunderstandings.

Conclusion

Improving our communication skills is essential to building strong, fulfilling relationships. By understanding the barriers that prevent us from effectively connecting with others and using strategies to overcome these barriers, we can deepen our connections and improve the quality of our personal and professional relationships. Remember, communication is a two-way street and it takes effort from both parties to make it work. Be patient, be open, and always strive to improve your communication skills.

11: The Impact of Technology on Relationships

The impact of technology on relationships cannot be overstated. In today's fast-paced world, technology has revolutionized the way we communicate and connect with others. On one hand, technology has made it easier to stay in touch with friends and family, no matter where they are in the world. On the other hand, it has also created new challenges and obstacles to building and maintaining healthy relationships. In this chapter, we will explore the ways in which technology affects relationships and how to use technology in a way that enhances, rather than detracts from, our connections with others.

One of the main ways that technology affects relationships is through our constant exposure to screens. Whether it's a phone, computer, or tablet, screens are an ever-present part of our lives. This constant exposure can lead to feelings of isolation, as we spend more time interacting with our devices than with the people around us. This can be particularly challenging for couples, who may find themselves constantly checking their phones instead of engaging with each other. It's important to be mindful of how much time you're spending on your devices, and to set aside dedicated time for face-to-face interaction with your partner.

Another challenge posed by technology is the impact it can have on our ability to communicate effectively. With text messaging, email, and social media, it's easy to misinterpret tone and meaning in written communication. This can lead to miscommunication, misunderstandings, and even hurt feelings. To overcome these challenges, it's important to be mindful of the way you communicate online, and to use clear and concise language whenever possible. If you're in doubt about the tone of a message, it's always best to pick up the phone and have a face-to-face conversation.

In addition to the challenges posed by technology, there are also many ways in which it can enhance our relationships. For example, social media can be a great way to stay connected with friends and family, even if you live far apart. With video conferencing and virtual reality technologies, it's now possible to have a face-to-face conversation with someone on the other side of the world. These technologies have made it easier to maintain long-distance relationships and to stay in touch with people who are important to us.

11: THE IMPACT OF TECHNOLOGY ON RELATIONSHIPS

In conclusion, technology has both positive and negative effects on relationships. While it's important to be mindful of the ways in which technology can detract from our connections with others, it's also important to embrace the positive aspects of technology and use it to enhance our relationships. Whether it's through setting aside dedicated time for face-to-face interaction, communicating effectively online, or using technology to stay connected with friends and family, there are many ways in which technology can help us build and maintain strong, healthy relationships.

12: The Importance of Quality Time: Building Strong Connections

Introduction:

Quality time is a valuable aspect of relationships that is often overlooked or taken for granted. It refers to the deliberate, intentional, and focused attention you give to someone else. Whether it is a romantic partner, family member, or friend, taking the time to truly be present and connect with those we care about is a key component of building strong and fulfilling relationships.

Why Quality Time Matters:

In today's fast-paced world, it is easy to get caught up in the demands of work, responsibilities, and other distractions. However, making quality time a priority in your relationships can have a profound impact on their health and longevity. Research has shown that people who prioritize quality time with their loved ones report greater levels of happiness, satisfaction, and overall well-being.

The Benefits of Quality Time:

12: THE IMPORTANCE OF QUALITY TIME: BUILDING STRONG CONNECTIONS

There are many benefits to dedicating quality time to your relationships. Some of these include:

– Improved Communication: Spending time together allows for open and honest communication, which can deepen understanding and increase intimacy.

– Strengthened Bonds: By investing time and effort into a relationship, you are demonstrating your commitment and strengthening the bond between you and your loved one.

– Reduced Stress: Spending quality time with others has been shown to reduce stress and improve mood.

– Better Problem-Solving: When you take the time to listen and understand the perspectives of others, you can better collaborate and solve problems together.

– Increased Happiness: Studies have found that people who spend more time with loved ones report greater levels of happiness and satisfaction.

How to Make Quality Time a Priority:

Making quality time a priority can seem challenging, but

there are simple steps you can take to ensure that it becomes a regular part of your relationships. Here are a few suggestions:

– Set aside time each week for quality time: This can be a regular date night, a family game night, or even just a coffee or phone call with a friend.

– Turn off technology: When spending quality time with someone, it is important to be present and focused. Turn off your phone, computer, and other distractions to be fully present with your loved one.

– Plan special experiences: Quality time doesn't have to be limited to just talking. Plan special experiences, such as a weekend getaway or a cooking class, to create meaningful memories with those you care about.

– Show appreciation: A simple "thank you" or a small gesture can go a long way in showing your loved ones that their time and presence is valued.

Conclusion:

Quality time is a critical component of strong and fulfilling relationships. By taking the time to be fully present and connect with those we care about, we can improve communication, strengthen bonds, reduce stress, and increase happiness. So, make quality time a priority in your relationships and start experiencing the many benefits it has to offer.

13: Understanding Love Languages: Enhancing Your Love Life

Introduction

The concept of love languages was introduced by Dr. Gary Chapman in his book "The 5 Love Languages: The Secret to Love That Lasts." In this chapter, we will delve deeper into the love languages and explore how they can enhance your love life. Understanding your love language, as well as your partner's, can help you improve communication, deepen your connection, and strengthen your relationship.

What are Love Languages?

Love languages are the ways in which individuals express and experience love. According to Dr. Chapman, there are five love languages: words of affirmation, acts of service, receiving gifts, physical touch, and quality time. These languages help us understand how we give and receive love, and how we can better meet our partner's needs.

Words of Affirmation

Individuals who have words of affirmation as their love language thrive on hearing positive words from their partner.

They feel loved when their partner compliments them, tells them how much they mean to them, or expresses appreciation for them. To show love to someone who values words of affirmation, it's important to speak kind words and offer verbal affirmations often.

Acts of Service

Individuals who have acts of service as their love language feel loved when their partner helps them out with chores, errands, or tasks. Doing things for your partner that they would typically have to do themselves, such as cooking dinner or doing laundry, shows them that you care and are willing to put effort into the relationship. This love language is all about actions, and not just words.

Receiving Gifts

For individuals who have receiving gifts as their love language, giving and receiving gifts is a tangible expression of love. It's not about the cost of the gift, but rather the thought behind it. Even small, thoughtful gifts can mean a lot to someone whose love language is receiving gifts.

13: UNDERSTANDING LOVE LANGUAGES: ENHANCING YOUR LOVE LIFE

Physical Touch

Individuals who have physical touch as their love language feel loved when their partner touches them in a affectionate way, such as holding hands, cuddling, or hugging. Physical touch can help strengthen the emotional bond between partners, and is an important aspect of love for those who value this love language.

Quality Time

Individuals who have quality time as their love language feel loved when their partner gives them undivided attention. This means putting away distractions, such as phones or laptops, and truly being present in the moment. Spending quality time with your partner can be as simple as going for a walk or having a deep conversation over a cup of coffee.

Conclusion

Knowing and understanding your love language, as well as your partner's, can greatly enhance your relationship. By learning how to give and receive love in ways that resonate with each other, you can deepen your connection, improve communication, and build a lasting, fulfilling relationship. Take the time to identify your love language, and use this information to strengthen your relationships and bring more love and happiness into your life.

14: Relationships and Self-Esteem: Building Confidence and Empowerment

Introduction:

Self-esteem plays a critical role in our relationships, both personal and professional. A high level of self-esteem can enhance our interactions and lead to more fulfilling connections. On the other hand, low self-esteem can be a barrier to healthy relationships and can lead to self-doubt, insecurity, and negative self-talk. In this chapter, we will explore the connection between self-esteem and relationships, and provide strategies for building confidence and empowerment in your interactions with others.

The Connection between Self-Esteem and Relationships:

Self-esteem is defined as our overall sense of worth and value as a person. It is shaped by our experiences and the messages we receive from others, as well as our internal self-talk. A high level of self-esteem can lead to positive relationships, as individuals with high self-esteem are more likely to feel confident in themselves and their interactions with others. They are less likely to be affected by negative

43

comments or criticism, and are more likely to engage in healthy relationships.

Low self-esteem, on the other hand, can negatively impact relationships. Individuals with low self-esteem may struggle with self-doubt and insecurity, which can lead to negative self-talk and poor communication skills. They may also be more susceptible to criticism, leading to further feelings of worthlessness and a negative cycle of self-doubt. This can result in strained relationships and missed opportunities for fulfilling connections.

Building Confidence and Empowerment:

There are several strategies for building self-esteem and enhancing your relationships. These include:

— Practice positive self-talk: Reframing negative thoughts and replacing them with positive affirmations can help to build confidence and self-esteem.

— Surround yourself with positive people: Surrounding yourself with supportive individuals who uplift and encourage you can help to boost your self-esteem and improve your relationships.

– Focus on your strengths: Instead of focusing on your weaknesses, focus on your strengths and the things that make you unique. This can help to build confidence and enhance your relationships.

– Engage in self-care: Taking care of yourself physically and mentally can help to build self-esteem and improve your relationships. Engage in activities that make you feel good and focus on your overall well-being.

– Seek support from a professional: If you are struggling with low self-esteem, seeking the support of a professional counselor or therapist can be helpful. They can provide personalized strategies for building self-esteem and enhancing your relationships.

Conclusion:

Self-esteem plays a critical role in our relationships, and it is important to focus on building confidence and empowerment. By using the strategies outlined in this chapter, you can improve your self-esteem and enhance your personal and professional relationships. Remember, building self-esteem takes time and effort, but the rewards of positive, fulfilling connections are worth it.

15: The Power of Positive Affirmations: Transforming Your Relationships

Positive affirmations have the power to transform the way you think, feel, and interact with others. When you repeat positive affirmations, you are essentially reprogramming your mind to think more positively, which can have a profound impact on your relationships.

Whether you're struggling with low self-esteem, negative thoughts, or conflict in your relationships, positive affirmations can help you overcome these challenges and build stronger, more fulfilling connections.

To start using positive affirmations, simply choose a statement that resonates with you, and repeat it to yourself throughout the day. For example, if you struggle with self-doubt, you might repeat the affirmation, "I am worthy of love and respect." If you struggle with conflict in your relationships, you might repeat the affirmation, "I communicate with compassion and understanding."

Positive affirmations can be especially powerful when used in combination with other relationship-building techniques, such as active listening, setting healthy boundaries, and practicing emotional intelligence.

In addition to repeating affirmations, you can also write them down, post them in a visible place, or even set them as a daily reminder on your phone. The more you repeat these affirmations, the more they will become a part of your thoughts and beliefs, and the more they will influence your relationships.

Positive affirmations are a simple yet powerful tool for transforming your relationships. By repeating them regularly, you can change the way you think and feel, and ultimately build stronger, more fulfilling connections with others.

16: Understanding Your Partner: Building Empathy and Connection

Introduction:

In order to build strong and fulfilling relationships, it is essential to understand and appreciate the perspective and experiences of our partner. Understanding your partner involves building empathy and a deep connection that allows you to see the world through their eyes. In this chapter, we will explore the various ways in which you can better understand your partner and build a more connected relationship.

Building Empathy:

Empathy is the ability to understand and share the feelings of another person. When you are able to put yourself in your partner's shoes and see things from their perspective, you are able to build a deeper level of connection and understanding. This can be achieved through active listening, asking questions, and paying attention to nonverbal cues.

Active Listening:

Active listening involves not just hearing what your partner is saying, but also fully engaging with and understanding their words. This involves paying attention, not interrupting, and asking questions to clarify what they are saying. By actively listening to your partner, you can gain a deeper understanding of their thoughts and feelings, and build a stronger connection.

Nonverbal Cues:

Nonverbal cues, such as body language, facial expressions, and tone of voice, can often reveal more about someone's feelings and thoughts than their words alone. Paying attention to these cues can give you a deeper understanding of your partner and help you build a more connected relationship.

Asking Questions:

Asking questions is a powerful tool for understanding your partner. By asking questions, you can gain insight into their thoughts, feelings, and experiences, and build a deeper connection. However, it is important to ask questions in a nonjudgmental and open-minded way, and to truly listen to the answers.

16: UNDERSTANDING YOUR PARTNER: BUILDING EMPATHY AND CONNECTION

Putting it into Practice:

In order to build a deep and connected relationship, it is important to consistently put these practices into action. This may involve making a conscious effort to listen more actively, pay attention to nonverbal cues, and ask questions. It may also involve setting aside time for intentional conversations where you can focus on understanding your partner.

Conclusion:

By understanding your partner, you can build a deeper level of connection and empathy that is essential for a fulfilling and lasting relationship. By incorporating active listening, paying attention to nonverbal cues, and asking questions, you can gain a deeper understanding of your partner and build a more connected relationship. Remember that building understanding takes time and effort, but the rewards are well worth it.

17: Relationships and Mental Health: Navigating Emotional Well-Being

In this chapter, we will be exploring the important role that mental health plays in relationships. Mental health refers to our emotional, psychological, and social well-being, and it greatly impacts our ability to form and maintain healthy relationships.

One of the biggest challenges when it comes to mental health and relationships is managing the stigma that still exists around mental illness. Many people are hesitant to seek help or even talk about their mental health struggles because they fear being judged or misunderstood. However, it's important to understand that mental health conditions are common and treatable, and seeking help is a sign of strength, not weakness.

When it comes to relationships, mental health can impact everything from communication and conflict resolution to intimacy and emotional connection. For example, depression or anxiety can make it difficult for someone to express their feelings or engage in social activities, which can strain relationships. On the other hand, untreated mental health conditions can also lead to behaviors that are harmful to relationships, such as anger or substance abuse.

To build healthy relationships and maintain emotional well-being, it's important to take care of your mental health. This can include seeking professional help, practicing self-care, and developing healthy coping strategies. It's also important to educate yourself about mental health conditions and understand that they don't define who someone is.

It's also crucial to have open and honest communication with your partner about your mental health. This can help build understanding and empathy, and also prevent misunderstandings and conflicts. If your partner is struggling with a mental health condition, it's important to offer support and encouragement to seek professional help.

In addition, it's essential to be aware of the impact that relationships can have on mental health. Relationships can be a source of comfort, support, and happiness, but they can also be a source of stress and conflict. It's important to have healthy boundaries, communicate openly, and seek professional help when necessary.

17: RELATIONSHIPS AND MENTAL HEALTH: NAVIGATING EMOTIONAL WELL-BEING

In conclusion, mental health is an important aspect of relationships, and taking care of it is crucial for building lasting, fulfilling connections. By seeking help, educating yourself, and engaging in open communication with your partner, you can navigate the challenges and reap the benefits of healthy relationships.

18: Finding Love: Tips for Meeting Your Perfect Partner

Finding love can often feel like an elusive and elusive experience, but with the right tools and mindset, it can be a fulfilling and joyful journey. Whether you are looking for a romantic relationship, a close friendship, or a professional connection, the process of finding love begins with understanding what you are looking for and what is important to you.

One of the most important things to consider when looking for love is to have a clear understanding of who you are and what you want. This requires self-reflection and self-awareness, which can be achieved through activities such as journaling, meditation, or therapy. When you have a clear understanding of yourself, you are better able to communicate your needs, values, and boundaries to others, which is critical in attracting and maintaining healthy relationships.

Another key factor in finding love is to cultivate a positive attitude. Instead of focusing on what you lack in your life or what you hope to gain from a relationship, focus on the good things in your life and the things you have to offer others. Cultivating gratitude and positivity can help you attract people who are positive and who value the same things that you do.

It is also important to be open to new experiences and to take risks in your search for love. This means stepping outside of your comfort zone, trying new things, and being open to meeting new people. Joining clubs or groups that align with your interests, volunteering, or taking classes in a subject you are passionate about are great ways to meet new people and find love.

Networking is another great way to meet new people and find love. Attend events, join online communities, and connect with people in your professional and social networks. The more people you meet, the more opportunities you have to find someone who is compatible with you.

When you meet someone new, it is important to be yourself and to be open and honest about your intentions. Don't pretend to be someone you're not, or try to hide parts of yourself, as this will only lead to disappointment and misunderstandings in the long run. Be yourself, be genuine, and be honest about what you are looking for in a relationship.

18: FINDING LOVE: TIPS FOR MEETING YOUR PERFECT PARTNER

Another important aspect of finding love is to be patient. Love often takes time, and it may take several attempts to find the right person. Don't be discouraged if your first few attempts don't lead to lasting relationships, and don't give up if things don't work out right away. Keep putting yourself out there and stay positive, and eventually, you will find someone who is the right fit for you.

Finally, it is important to maintain healthy habits and a positive self-image, as this will attract the right people into your life. Take care of yourself physically, mentally, and emotionally, and cultivate a strong sense of self-worth. This will help you attract people who appreciate and value you for who you are, and who will support and encourage you in your search for love.

In conclusion, finding love is a journey that requires self-reflection, a positive attitude, openness to new experiences, networking, honesty, patience, and self-care. By following these tips, you can increase your chances of finding the love and connection you seek, and transform your relationships for the better.

19: Maintaining a Fulfilling Relationship: The Keys to Lasting Love

A fulfilling relationship is one that brings joy, comfort, and a sense of security to both partners. While many people believe that love is enough to sustain a relationship, the truth is that it takes much more than just love to make a relationship last. Relationships require effort, communication, and understanding from both partners in order to grow and flourish. In this chapter, we will explore the keys to maintaining a fulfilling relationship that can stand the test of time.

– Communication is Key

Communication is the foundation of any healthy relationship. It is important to have open and honest conversations with your partner about your feelings, wants, and needs. When you communicate with your partner, be sure to listen to them with empathy and understanding. Avoid interrupting or talking over them, and instead focus on what they are saying and how you can support them.

In addition to having open and honest conversations, it is also important to have regular check-ins with your partner.

Ask them how they are feeling and if there is anything you can do to support them. Make sure to take the time to listen to their response, and be open to hearing about their concerns or needs.

– Respect Each Other's Differences

In any relationship, there are bound to be differences between partners. It is important to respect each other's unique perspectives, beliefs, and values. Try to understand where your partner is coming from and why they feel the way they do. This can help you to have more productive and positive conversations, and can also help to prevent conflicts from escalating.

– Keep the Romance Alive

It is important to keep the romance alive in your relationship. Plan special dates, surprise your partner with thoughtful gestures, and take the time to connect and build intimacy. Whether it's a candlelit dinner or a weekend getaway, taking the time to nurture your relationship will help you both to feel more connected and fulfilled.

19: MAINTAINING A FULFILLING RELATIONSHIP: THE KEYS TO LASTING LOVE

– Show Appreciation and Gratitude

Make sure to show appreciation and gratitude for your partner on a regular basis. Take the time to acknowledge and appreciate the things that they do for you, and be sure to let them know that you are grateful for their love and support. This will help you to maintain a positive and supportive relationship and will strengthen your bond over time.

– Find Balance

It is important to find balance in your relationship. This means making time for both your relationship and individual interests and pursuits. Encourage your partner to pursue their own interests, and be supportive of their goals and aspirations. By finding balance, you will be able to maintain a healthy and fulfilling relationship that lasts.

– Embrace Change

Change is a natural part of life, and it is important to embrace it in your relationship. Be open to new experiences, and be willing to adapt and grow together. By being open to change, you will be able to evolve and strengthen your rela-

19: MAINTAINING A FULFILLING RELATIONSHIP: THE KEYS TO LASTING LOVE

tionship over time.

In conclusion, maintaining a fulfilling relationship takes effort, communication, and understanding from both partners. By following these keys to lasting love, you can build and sustain a relationship that brings joy, comfort, and a sense of security to both partners. So, make sure to keep these tips in mind and apply them in your own relationship to unlock the secrets to lasting love, fulfilling connections, and happy relationships.

20: Understanding Intimacy: Enhancing Physical and Emotional Connections

Intimacy is a crucial aspect of relationships, as it helps to foster emotional and physical closeness and strengthens the bond between partners. The development of intimacy is a gradual process that can be enhanced through communication, empathy, and shared experiences.

Physical intimacy refers to the physical expressions of love and affection, such as holding hands, cuddling, and sexual activity. This type of intimacy can greatly enhance the emotional connection between partners and increase feelings of trust and security.

However, it is important to recognize that physical intimacy is not the only aspect of a relationship, and should never be forced or coerced. Instead, it should be a mutual decision made between partners, and should always involve clear communication and mutual consent.

Emotional intimacy refers to the sharing of feelings, thoughts, and experiences between partners. This type of intimacy requires vulnerability and trust, and involves sharing personal stories, expressing feelings, and opening up to each other. Emotional intimacy can greatly enhance the overall relationship, as it helps partners to better understand and support each other.

In order to enhance intimacy in relationships, it is important to prioritize communication and empathy. This includes actively listening to each other, expressing empathy, and being open and honest about your feelings and thoughts. Additionally, taking the time to engage in shared experiences and activities can also help to foster intimacy and deepen the emotional connection between partners.

It is also important to recognize that intimacy can sometimes be impacted by external factors, such as stress, physical and emotional health issues, and the impact of technology on relationships. In these situations, it is important to address these challenges together, and to prioritize communication and empathy to maintain a strong and fulfilling intimate connection.

In conclusion, intimacy is a critical aspect of relationships, and is essential for fostering a strong emotional and physical connection between partners. By prioritizing commu-

nication, empathy, and shared experiences, partners can
enhance intimacy and build a lasting and fulfilling relationship.

21: Navigating Relationships in the Workplace: Building Professional Connections

Introduction

The workplace is a unique environment where individuals from diverse backgrounds come together to achieve a common goal. In this environment, it is important to develop and maintain positive relationships with coworkers, supervisors, and subordinates. Strong relationships in the workplace can lead to improved communication, increased productivity, and a more enjoyable work experience. On the other hand, negative relationships can result in decreased morale, decreased productivity, and a hostile work environment. This chapter will explore the various types of relationships that can exist in the workplace and provide strategies for building and maintaining positive relationships.

Types of Relationships in the Workplace

There are several different types of relationships that can exist in the workplace, including:

– Coworker relationships: These are relationships between individuals who work in the same department or on the same team.

– Supervisor/subordinate relationships: These relationships exist between a supervisor and the individuals who report to them.

– Cross-functional relationships: These relationships exist between individuals from different departments or teams who need to collaborate to achieve a common goal.

– Customer/vendor relationships: These relationships exist between individuals who work for the company and external customers or vendors.

Building Positive Relationships in the Workplace

There are several strategies that can be used to build and maintain positive relationships in the workplace. Some of these strategies include:

– Open and honest communication: Clear and open communication is essential for building positive relationships in the workplace. This involves listening to others, being respectful, and avoiding making assumptions.

– Building trust: Trust is a key component of any relationship, and it can be built through consistent and reliable behavior, as well as transparency and honesty.

– Showing appreciation: Expressing gratitude and acknowledging the contributions of others can help to build positive relationships in the workplace.

– Being respectful: Treating others with respect and dignity, even in challenging situations, is essential for building positive relationships in the workplace.

– Team building activities: Engaging in team building activities, such as team-building exercises, can help to build relationships and improve communication among team members.

Maintaining Positive Relationships in the Workplace

Once positive relationships have been established in the workplace, it is important to maintain them. Some strategies for maintaining positive relationships include:

– Being flexible: Being willing to adapt and adjust to changing circumstances and the needs of others is essential for maintaining positive relationships in the workplace.

– Being positive: Maintaining a positive attitude and outlook can help to maintain positive relationships in the workplace, even in challenging situations.

– Providing support: Providing support and assistance to others, especially in times of need, can help to strengthen relationships in the workplace.

– Being proactive: Proactively addressing potential conflicts and issues, before they become major problems, can help to maintain positive relationships in the workplace.

Conclusion

Relationships in the workplace play a critical role in determining the overall success and happiness of individuals in the workplace. By understanding the different types of relationships that can exist in the workplace, and by utilizing strategies for building and maintaining positive relationships, individuals can create a work environment that is positive, productive, and fulfilling. Whether working with coworkers, supervisors, customers, or vendors, developing positive relationships is essential for achieving success and happiness in the workplace.

22: Managing Relationships with Friends and Family: Maintaining Strong Personal Ties

Relationships with friends and family are some of the most important connections we have in our lives. They provide us with support, comfort, and a sense of belonging that is unmatched. However, these relationships can also be some of the most challenging, as close connections can sometimes lead to conflict, hurt, and disappointment.

In order to maintain strong personal ties with friends and family, it is important to understand the dynamics of these relationships and to work towards building and maintaining a positive, healthy connection. Here are some tips and strategies for navigating relationships with friends and family:

– Communication is key: Communication is the foundation of any healthy relationship. It is important to regularly check in with friends and family members, to listen actively, and to be open and honest about your feelings and thoughts. When conflicts arise, it is important to approach them with a calm and constructive attitude, and to be willing to find a resolution that works for everyone involved.

– Set boundaries: Maintaining a healthy relationship with friends and family members requires setting clear boundaries. This means understanding your own needs and limitations, and being clear about what you are comfortable with and what you are not. This can help you avoid burnout, maintain your emotional well-being, and prevent conflicts from arising in the first place.

– Practice forgiveness: Forgiveness is a powerful tool in maintaining strong personal relationships with friends and family. When conflicts do arise, it is important to be willing to let go of anger and resentment, and to work towards finding a resolution that is beneficial for everyone involved. Forgiving others does not mean that you are condoning their behavior, but rather, it means that you are choosing to move forward and to focus on maintaining a positive connection.

– Embrace vulnerability: Maintaining strong personal relationships requires being vulnerable and opening up to others. This means sharing your thoughts, feelings, and experiences, and being open to receiving feedback from friends and family members. When we are open and vulnerable, we build stronger connections and foster greater understanding and empathy.

– Prioritize quality time: Spending quality time with friends and family members is an important part of building and maintaining strong personal relationships. Whether it's going for a walk, having a meal together, or just sitting down for a chat, taking the time to connect with those you care about can help strengthen your bond and foster greater understanding and empathy.

– Celebrate successes: Celebrating the successes and milestones of friends and family members is an important way of building and maintaining strong personal relationships. Whether it's a new job, a promotion, or a personal accomplishment, taking the time to acknowledge and celebrate these milestones can help build a stronger bond and foster a positive connection.

– Be there for each other: Supporting and being there for friends and family members during difficult times is an important aspect of maintaining strong personal relationships. Whether it's lending a listening ear, offering a helping hand, or just being there to provide support, being there for those we care about is a powerful way of building a positive and healthy connection.

In conclusion, maintaining strong personal relationships with friends and family members requires a commitment to building and maintaining positive, healthy connections. Whether it's through regular communication, setting clear boundaries, embracing vulnerability, or simply being there for each other, taking the time to invest in these relationships can lead to lasting love, fulfilling connections, and happy relationships.

23: Dealing with Jealousy and Envy in Relationships

Jealousy and envy are two of the most destructive emotions that can sabotage even the strongest relationships. While it is natural to feel jealous or envious at times, it is important to understand the root cause of these emotions and learn how to manage them in a healthy way. This chapter will explore the difference between jealousy and envy, the causes of these emotions, and the steps you can take to overcome them.

Jealousy is an intense emotion that is usually triggered by the fear of losing someone or something that you value. For example, if you are in a romantic relationship and you become aware of someone who seems to be paying attention to your partner, you might start to feel jealous. Similarly, if you have a close friend who seems to be spending more time with someone else, you might also experience jealousy.

Envy, on the other hand, is an emotion that is often triggered by feelings of inadequacy and a desire to have what others have. For example, if you see someone with a better job, a nicer car, or a more fulfilling relationship, you might start to feel envious. Unlike jealousy, envy is more focused on what someone else has, rather than the fear of losing something that you already have.

The root cause of jealousy and envy is often related to low self-esteem and a lack of self-worth. If you do not feel good about yourself, it can be easy to become jealous or envious of others who seem to have what you lack. Additionally, these emotions can also be fueled by comparisons to others and a constant need to measure up to others' achievements and possessions.

To overcome jealousy and envy in your relationships, it is important to start by building a strong sense of self-worth and confidence. This can be achieved by focusing on your own strengths, accomplishments, and values, and by surrounding yourself with positive and supportive people.

It is also important to practice gratitude and to focus on the good things in your life. By focusing on what you have, rather than what you lack, you will start to feel more content and satisfied with your life. This, in turn, will help to reduce feelings of jealousy and envy.

It can also be helpful to set boundaries and to avoid comparing yourself to others. This means avoiding people and situations that trigger these emotions, and instead focusing on what is important to you and what makes you happy.

Finally, it is important to communicate openly and honestly with your partner or friends when you are feeling jealous or envious. By talking about your feelings, you can work together to find a solution that will help you to feel more secure and satisfied in your relationship.

In conclusion, jealousy and envy are natural emotions that can be overcome with self-awareness, self-reflection, and effective communication. By learning how to manage these emotions in a healthy way, you can build stronger, more fulfilling relationships that are based on trust, respect, and love.

24: The Impact of Childhood Experiences on Relationships

Our childhood experiences have a profound impact on our relationships, shaping the way we interact with others and the patterns we tend to follow in our personal and professional lives. From the way we were treated by our caregivers, to the emotional environment of our childhood home, to our experiences with peers and authority figures, our early life experiences help to form our beliefs and behaviors.

For many people, negative childhood experiences can lead to low self-esteem, trust issues, and difficulties in forming meaningful relationships. On the other hand, positive experiences in childhood can lay the foundation for healthy, fulfilling relationships in adulthood.

For example, those who experienced a childhood filled with love, support, and stability tend to have higher self-esteem and better interpersonal skills. They tend to approach relationships with a positive outlook and have a greater capacity for intimacy and emotional openness. They are also more likely to have healthy communication skills and the ability to resolve conflicts in a productive manner.

24: THE IMPACT OF CHILDHOOD EXPERIENCES ON RELATIONSHIPS

On the other hand, individuals who experienced emotional, physical, or sexual abuse in childhood may struggle with trust, emotional intimacy, and maintaining healthy relationships. They may also experience anxiety, depression, and other mental health issues that can impact their ability to form meaningful connections with others.

It is important to recognize the impact of childhood experiences on our relationships and to seek help if necessary. Therapy, support groups, and self-help resources can be useful in addressing negative patterns and healing from childhood traumas. With the right tools and support, it is possible to transform our relationships and create the fulfilling connections we deserve.

Additionally, it is important to be mindful of the impact of our own experiences on our children and to strive to create a positive and supportive environment for them. By fostering healthy relationships in our own homes, we can help to break the cycle of negativity and set the next generation on a path towards fulfilling connections.

In conclusion, understanding the impact of childhood experiences on relationships is crucial to creating and maintaining healthy, fulfilling connections in our personal and professional lives. By acknowledging the influence of our past and seeking help where necessary, we can work towards transforming our relationships and building the love and connection we desire.

25: Healing from a Breakup: Moving Forward from Heartache

Introduction

Breaking up is never easy, and it can leave you feeling heartbroken, lonely, and lost. But it is important to remember that you are not alone and that with time and support, you can heal from a breakup and move forward in a positive direction. This chapter is designed to provide you with the tools and insights you need to process your emotions, heal from a breakup, and find happiness once again.

The Grief Process

The first step in healing from a breakup is to understand and accept the grief process. This process is natural and normal, and it involves a range of emotions that can include shock, anger, sadness, and guilt. It is important to allow yourself to experience these emotions, rather than trying to suppress or ignore them.

One way to process your emotions is to write them down in a journal. This can help you to understand and release the feelings that are causing you pain, and it can also provide you with a sense of closure. Additionally, talking to a trusted friend or therapist can provide you with a safe and supportive space to express your emotions and receive support.

Rebuilding Your Self-Esteem

Breaking up can take a toll on your self-esteem, leaving you feeling rejected and unworthy. It is important to work on rebuilding your self-esteem by focusing on your strengths, accomplishments, and the things you love about yourself. Engage in activities that you enjoy and that make you feel good about yourself, such as exercising, reading, or spending time with friends.

Setting Boundaries

In the aftermath of a breakup, it can be tempting to reach out to your ex and try to reconcile. However, this can prolong the healing process and prevent you from moving forward. It is important to set boundaries with your ex and avoid contact until you have processed your emotions and are ready to move on.

Letting Go of the Past

25: HEALING FROM A BREAKUP: MOVING FORWARD FROM HEARTACHE

Moving on from a breakup requires letting go of the past and focusing on the present and future. This can be difficult, but it is essential for your healing and growth. Try to avoid dwelling on the past and instead focus on the things that bring you joy and happiness.

Finding New Love

When you are ready, you may be interested in finding new love. This can be a scary and exciting experience, but it is important to approach it with patience and an open heart. Be open to new experiences and take the time to get to know someone before jumping into a relationship.

Conclusion

Healing from a breakup is a process, and it can take time and effort. But by understanding the grief process, rebuilding your self-esteem, setting boundaries, letting go of the past, and finding new love, you can transform your heartache into happiness and move forward in a positive direction. With the right support and guidance, you can unlock the secrets to lasting love, fulfilling connections, and happy relationships.

26: Relationships and Money: Managing Finances and Building Stronger Bonds

Introduction

Money and finances are a critical aspect of relationships and can often be a source of stress and tension between partners. Money is a tool that can be used to bring people together or tear them apart, depending on how it is managed. Understanding the impact of money on relationships is crucial for building strong, lasting connections with our partners and loved ones.

The Importance of Communication

One of the key elements of managing money in relationships is communication. It is essential to openly discuss financial goals, spending habits, and financial management strategies with your partner. This can help to avoid misunderstandings and conflicts that may arise from different perspectives on money management. It is also important to have regular financial check-ins to ensure that both partners are on the same page and that financial goals are being met.

26: RELATIONSHIPS AND MONEY: MANAGING FINANCES AND BUILDING STRONGER BONDS

Creating a Joint Budget

Creating a joint budget is an effective way to manage money in relationships. This involves combining the income and expenses of both partners into one budget, which can help to ensure that both partners are aware of the financial situation of the household. A joint budget can help to identify areas where expenses can be reduced, and it can also help to prioritize spending on items that are important to both partners. Additionally, a joint budget can provide a sense of accountability and transparency in financial management, which can help to build trust and strengthen the bond between partners.

Managing Debt

Debt is a common issue in many relationships and can cause significant stress and tension between partners. It is important to be honest about debt and to work together to create a plan to manage it. This may involve creating a budget to pay off debt, negotiating a payment plan with creditors, or seeking professional financial advice. The key is to approach debt as a team and to work together to find a solution that works for both partners.

26: RELATIONSHIPS AND MONEY: MANAGING FIN-ANCES AND BUILDING STRONGER BONDS

Planning for the Future

Planning for the future is an important aspect of managing money in relationships. This may involve setting financial goals, such as saving for retirement or buying a house, and creating a plan to achieve these goals. It is also important to have discussions about financial expectations, such as who will be responsible for paying bills or managing investments, and to make sure that both partners are on the same page. By working together to plan for the future, partners can ensure that they are both on track to achieve their financial goals and can build a stronger, more stable financial foundation for their relationship.

Conclusion

Managing money in relationships can be a challenging task, but it is also an opportunity to strengthen the bond between partners. By communicating openly and honestly, creating a joint budget, managing debt, and planning for the future, partners can work together to build a strong, financially secure relationship that will stand the test of time. Whether you are just starting a relationship or have been together for many years, it is never too late to start managing your finances in a way that will bring you closer together and help you build a brighter, more fulfilling future together.

27: Building Relationships with Children: Nurturing the Next Generation

Children are the future of the world and the future of our relationships. They are the ones who will carry on the legacy of love and connections that we build today. It is crucial that we provide them with the tools and skills necessary to build strong, healthy relationships in their own lives. In this chapter, we will discuss how to build relationships with children, the importance of nurturing the next generation, and how to help children develop the skills needed for lasting love, fulfilling connections, and happy relationships.

First, it is important to understand that building relationships with children is a two-way street. Children are not just passive recipients of our love and attention. They are active participants in the relationship, and they have their own needs, wants, and desires. This means that we must approach our relationships with children with empathy and understanding, taking into account their individual personalities, needs, and perspectives.

One of the most important things we can do to build relationships with children is to spend time with them. This can mean playing games, reading together, or simply talking. By spending time with children, we create a strong emotional bond that will last a lifetime. This time should also be quality time, where we are fully present and engaged in the activity or conversation. By being fully present, we show children that they are valued and that their thoughts and opinions matter.

Another key aspect of building relationships with children is communication. Good communication is the foundation of all strong relationships, and this is no different with children. We must learn to listen to children and understand what they are saying. This means actively engaging with them, asking questions, and encouraging them to express themselves. In turn, we must also be clear and concise in our own communication, ensuring that we are communicating our own thoughts, feelings, and expectations in a way that is easy for children to understand.

In addition to spending time with children and communication, building relationships with children also requires patience and understanding. Children are still developing their emotional and social skills, and they may not always respond in the way we expect or want them to. It is important that we remain patient and understanding, and that we continue to support and encourage them in their growth and development.

Another important aspect of building relationships with children is to provide them with a positive role model. Children learn by watching and imitating those around them, and it is our responsibility to set a good example. This means demonstrating healthy relationships, communication skills, and emotional intelligence in our own relationships. By doing so, we can help children develop these skills and traits in their own lives.

Finally, it is important to remember that building relationships with children is a lifelong process. As children grow and develop, their needs, wants, and perspectives will change. We must be willing to adapt and evolve our relationships with them, continuing to provide them with the support, love, and understanding they need as they grow into adulthood.

In conclusion, building relationships with children is a crucial aspect of nurturing the next generation and helping them develop the skills needed for lasting love, fulfilling connections, and happy relationships. By spending time with children, communicating effectively, being patient and understanding, providing a positive role model, and evolving our relationships with them over time, we can help them develop the skills they need to build strong, healthy relationships in their own lives.

28: Navigating Interpersonal Relationships: Tips for Building Positive Connections

Introduction

Interpersonal relationships are a crucial aspect of our lives. They are the foundation of our social, emotional, and professional well-being. The quality of our relationships with others can greatly influence our overall happiness and satisfaction in life. However, building and maintaining positive relationships is not always easy, especially in a world where we are constantly connected to one another through technology and social media.

In this chapter, we will explore tips for navigating interpersonal relationships, so you can build positive connections and foster lasting relationships with others. Whether it's with family members, friends, co-workers, or romantic partners, these tips will help you to communicate effectively, resolve conflicts, and build trust with those around you.

– Communication is key

28: NAVIGATING INTERPERSONAL RELATIONSHIPS: TIPS FOR BUILDING POSITIVE CONNECTIONS

Effective communication is the cornerstone of any strong relationship. When we communicate well, we are able to express our needs, listen to the needs of others, and work towards finding a solution that meets everyone's needs. To improve your communication skills, it's important to:

– Listen actively: Pay attention to what the other person is saying, and show that you are engaged in the conversation by nodding, making eye contact, and asking questions.

– Express yourself clearly: Be clear and concise when expressing your thoughts and feelings. Avoid using sarcasm or attacking language, as this can create unnecessary conflicts.

– Be open to feedback: Be open to hearing what others have to say about your communication style, and be willing to make changes if needed.

– Resolve conflicts in a positive manner

Conflict is inevitable in any relationship, but it's how we handle conflicts that can make or break a relationship. When resolving conflicts, it's important to:

– Remain calm: Take a step back from the situation and try

to calm down before addressing the conflict.

– Listen to each other: Allow both parties to express their perspective and actively listen to what the other person is saying.

– Find common ground: Work together to find a solution that meets both of your needs.

– Seek professional help: If conflicts persist and you are unable to resolve them on your own, consider seeking the help of a professional mediator or therapist.

– Show appreciation and gratitude

Expressing gratitude and appreciation can help build and strengthen relationships. Simple acts of kindness, like saying "thank you" or acknowledging someone's hard work, can go a long way in building trust and fostering positive relationships.

– Practice forgiveness

Forgiveness is a powerful tool in any relationship. When we forgive others, we release ourselves from the negative emotions associated with a situation and allow ourselves to move forward in a positive direction.

– Set boundaries

Setting clear boundaries is important in any relationship. It helps to establish mutual respect and ensures that both parties are on the same page. When setting boundaries, be clear about what is and isn't acceptable, and communicate these boundaries to others.

– Foster a positive attitude

Having a positive attitude can make a big difference in how we relate to others. When we approach relationships with a positive mindset, we are more likely to attract positive relationships into our lives and resolve conflicts in a more productive manner.

Conclusion

Building positive relationships requires effort and commitment, but the rewards are well worth it. By using the tips outlined in this chapter, you can develop stronger, more fulfilling connections with others, and enjoy happier, more satisfying relationships in all areas of your life. Whether it's with your romantic partner, family members, friends, or co-workers, remember that relationships are a two-way street, and it's up to each of us to make the effort to communicate effectively, resolve conflicts, and build trust with

29: Understanding and Managing Relationships in a Digital World

In recent years, the rise of technology and the internet has dramatically transformed the way we interact with one another. Today, it's common for people to form and maintain relationships through digital means, whether through social media, dating apps, or virtual communication. While this has made it easier for people to connect with others from all over the world, it has also raised new challenges in navigating relationships in a digital world.

One of the key challenges of relationships in a digital world is the prevalence of online deception and impersonation. People can easily create false identities and manipulate others online, leading to confusion, hurt, and even harm. To protect yourself in a digital world, it's important to be cautious and vigilant about the information you share online and the people you interact with. This may mean limiting your exposure to potentially harmful or deceptive individuals, or taking steps to verify the identities of those you meet online.

Another challenge of relationships in a digital world is the prevalence of distractions and interruptions. When we are constantly connected to the internet and our devices, it can be difficult to maintain focus and stay present in our relationships. This can result in feelings of disconnection and dissatisfaction, even with those we are closest to. To overcome these challenges, it's important to make time for face-to-face interaction and to establish healthy digital habits that promote connection and intimacy.

Despite these challenges, there are many benefits to relationships in a digital world. For example, it can be easier to meet people from diverse backgrounds and find like-minded individuals, opening up new opportunities for connection and growth. Additionally, technology can be a valuable tool for maintaining relationships, helping us stay in touch with loved ones even when we are separated by distance.

One of the keys to successful relationships in a digital world is balance. It's important to strike a balance between using technology to enhance our relationships and avoiding the pitfalls that come with relying too heavily on technology. This means being intentional about how we use technology and setting boundaries around its use in our relationships.

29: UNDERSTANDING AND MANAGING RELATION- SHIPS IN A DIGITAL WORLD

To build and maintain strong relationships in a digital world, it's also essential to focus on building trust and connection. This means being transparent, open, and honest in our communication, and actively seeking out opportunities to connect and grow together. Whether it's through virtual dates, virtual game nights, or other activities, it's important to prioritize quality time and shared experiences with the people we care about.

Ultimately, the key to navigating relationships in a digital world is to be mindful and intentional in our interactions. By being aware of the challenges and opportunities that come with technology and relationships, and by actively working to foster strong connections with others, we can unlock the secrets to lasting love, fulfilling connections, and happy relationships in a digital world.

30: Building Relationships with Colleagues: Enhancing Teamwork and Collaboration

In today's fast-paced and competitive work environment, having strong relationships with your colleagues is more important than ever. Good working relationships can help you be more productive, increase job satisfaction, and even lead to opportunities for career advancement. However, building and maintaining positive relationships with colleagues can be challenging, especially in a busy workplace where people are focused on meeting deadlines and achieving goals.

The good news is that by adopting certain habits and practices, you can enhance your relationships with your colleagues and promote teamwork and collaboration in the workplace. In this chapter, we'll explore some key tips and strategies for building successful relationships with your colleagues.

– Be Respectful and Professional

The first step in building positive relationships with your colleagues is to be respectful and professional in your interactions with them. This means showing up on time, following workplace protocols, and treating everyone with dignity and respect, regardless of their position or status.

When communicating with your colleagues, it's important to be clear, concise, and professional. Avoid gossiping or spreading rumors, and be mindful of the tone of your messages, both written and spoken. If you have a disagreement with someone, approach it in a constructive and respectful manner, focusing on finding solutions rather than assigning blame.

– Show Interest in Your Colleagues' Lives

Another important aspect of building relationships with your colleagues is showing interest in their lives. Take the time to get to know your colleagues and learn about their interests, hobbies, and families. This can help build a deeper connection and foster a more positive work environment.

Showing interest in your colleagues doesn't have to mean that you need to become best friends, but it can be as simple as asking them how their weekend was or inquiring about a project they're working on. By taking an active interest in your colleagues' lives, you can help create a supportive work environment where everyone feels valued and appreciated.

– Be a Good Listener

Being a good listener is another essential component of building positive relationships with your colleagues. When someone is speaking to you, give them your full attention and listen carefully to what they're saying. This shows that you value their perspective and are interested in their thoughts and ideas.

Good listening also involves asking questions and being open to feedback. By actively engaging with your colleagues and taking the time to understand their perspectives, you can build stronger relationships and promote collaboration in the workplace.

– Be a Team Player

In today's fast-paced work environment, teamwork and collaboration are key to success. To build positive relationships with your colleagues, you need to be a team player who is willing to work together and support one another.

This can involve taking on additional responsibilities, helping others with their work, and being flexible when needed. It also means being willing to admit your mistakes and work together to find solutions when things go wrong. By working together as a team, you can build trust and respect with your colleagues, which is essential for positive working relationships.

– Share Your Expertise

Finally, to build positive relationships with your colleagues, it's important to share your expertise and skills. This means being willing to help others when they need it and offering constructive feedback and suggestions.

Sharing your expertise can help build trust and respect with your colleagues, and it can also help you develop new skills and build your professional network. By working together and sharing your knowledge and skills, you can help create a supportive work environment that promotes teamwork and collaboration.

30: BUILDING RELATIONSHIPS WITH COLLEAGUES: ENHANCING TEAMWORK AND COLLABORATION

In this chapter, we will explore the various ways in which you can build positive relationships with your colleagues and enhance teamwork and collaboration in the workplace. In today's fast-paced, highly competitive world, effective teamwork and collaboration are essential for success. Whether you're working on a project with a team of people, or simply interacting with your colleagues on a daily basis, building strong relationships with your coworkers can help create a positive and productive work environment.

One key factor in building relationships with your colleagues is communication. Good communication skills are essential in order to effectively collaborate with others and resolve conflicts. Make sure you listen actively, ask questions, and express your thoughts and opinions in a clear and respectful manner. Regular check-ins with your team can also help to build trust and foster a sense of collaboration.

Another way to build positive relationships with your colleagues is to be respectful and considerate of their needs and opinions. This includes taking the time to understand each other's perspectives, and being open to feedback and constructive criticism. Showing appreciation for your colleagues' contributions and hard work can also help to build a positive work environment.

In order to enhance teamwork and collaboration in the workplace, it is also important to establish clear goals and expectations for each project or task. This will help to ensure that everyone is working towards the same objectives, and that everyone understands their role in the process. Encouraging open and honest communication, and providing opportunities for team members to share their thoughts and ideas, can also help to foster a sense of teamwork and collaboration.

Finally, it is important to acknowledge and celebrate successes and achievements, both individually and as a team. Celebrating successes, no matter how small, can help to build morale and motivation, and encourage people to work even harder towards future successes.

In conclusion, building strong relationships with your colleagues and enhancing teamwork and collaboration in the workplace can lead to a more positive and productive work environment. By following the tips and strategies outlined in this chapter, you can develop the skills and techniques needed to build successful and fulfilling relationships with your coworkers.

31: Dealing with Difficult People: Strategies for Positive Interactions

Introduction:

Difficult people are a reality in both personal and professional relationships. They can be challenging to deal with, causing stress and negativity in our interactions. However, it's essential to understand that everyone has their own set of experiences and perspectives that shape their behavior. By understanding and addressing the underlying causes of their behavior, we can learn how to positively interact with even the most challenging individuals. In this chapter, we'll explore the different types of difficult people, the reasons behind their behavior, and practical strategies for managing positive relationships.

Types of Difficult People:

– The Negative Nelly: This type of person is always complaining and sees the glass as half-empty. They spread negativity, and it's challenging to have a positive interaction with them.

31: DEALING WITH DIFFICULT PEOPLE: STRATEGIES FOR POSITIVE INTERACTIONS

– The Know-it-All: This type of person thinks they have all the answers, and their opinions are always right. They can be condescending and dismissive of others' ideas.

– The Drama Queen: This type of person thrives on drama and conflict. They enjoy being the center of attention and can cause stress and tension in their relationships.

– The Passive-Aggressive: This type of person expresses their anger and frustration indirectly through sarcasm or avoiding communication.

– The Controlling: This type of person likes to have control over every aspect of their relationships, including the thoughts and actions of others.

Reasons Behind Difficult Behavior:

It's essential to understand that difficult behavior is often a manifestation of deeper issues. Some common reasons behind difficult behavior include:

– Fear of rejection or abandonment

– Low self-esteem and insecurity

— A history of trauma or abuse

— Unresolved past conflicts or relationship issues

— Mental health problems such as anxiety, depression, or personality disorders

Strategies for Positive Interactions:

— Practice Empathy: Try to understand the other person's perspective, and acknowledge their feelings.

— Set Boundaries: Establish clear and firm boundaries with the person. Be clear about what behavior is and is not acceptable to you.

— Communicate Openly: Be honest and direct in your communication with the person. Avoid passive-aggression and try to have open and honest conversations.

— Seek Help: If you're struggling to manage the relationship, consider seeking professional help, such as therapy or counseling.

— Take Care of Yourself: Remember to prioritize self-care,

and don't allow the difficult person to consume all of your energy and time.

Conclusion:

Dealing with difficult people can be challenging, but it's essential to remember that everyone has their own set of experiences that shape their behavior. By understanding the reasons behind their behavior and utilizing practical strategies, we can learn how to positively interact with even the most challenging individuals. Whether in personal or professional relationships, developing positive interactions with those around us is crucial for building fulfilling connections and fostering happiness in our lives.

32: The Role of Humor in Relationships: Laughing Your Way to Happiness

In a world filled with stress, deadlines, and responsibilities, laughter can be the best medicine for many of us. The same can be said for relationships. Humor can be a powerful tool in bringing people closer together, making difficult conversations easier, and just generally making life more enjoyable. In this chapter, we will explore the role that humor can play in relationships, why it's important, and how you can incorporate it into your personal and professional connections.

Humor Brings People Closer Together

Laughter is contagious, and when we share a good laugh with someone, it creates an instant bond. When we laugh with someone, we release endorphins, the body's natural "feel good" chemicals, which can make us feel more relaxed, happy, and connected to the person we're with. Humor also has a way of putting people at ease, and when we're relaxed and feeling good, it's much easier to have open and honest conversations.

32: THE ROLE OF HUMOR IN RELATIONSHIPS: LAUGHING YOUR WAY TO HAPPINESS

Humor Can Improve Communication

Humor can also play a crucial role in improving communication between partners. When people are able to laugh and joke with each other, it helps to break down barriers and reduces tensions. For example, if there's a sensitive topic that needs to be discussed, using humor can help to diffuse the situation and make it easier for both parties to express their feelings. Additionally, humor can help to create a more positive and relaxed atmosphere in which both parties feel more comfortable sharing their thoughts and feelings.

Humor Can Help to Resolve Conflicts

Humor can also be a powerful tool in resolving conflicts in relationships. When tensions are high and emotions are running high, it can be difficult to find common ground and resolve an issue. However, when humor is used to diffuse the situation, it can help to lighten the mood and put both parties in a better place to find a solution. For example, if you and your partner are having a disagreement about something, finding a way to make each other laugh can help to defuse the situation and create an environment in which both parties are more open to finding a solution.

32: THE ROLE OF HUMOR IN RELATIONSHIPS: LAUGHING YOUR WAY TO HAPPINESS

How to Incorporate Humor into Your Relationships

So, how can you incorporate humor into your relationships? There are a few key things to keep in mind:

– Be yourself: The most important thing is to be yourself and let your humor come out naturally. If you try to be someone you're not or force humor into a situation that doesn't naturally lend itself to it, it can come across as awkward or insincere.

– Find common ground: Find what you both find funny and focus on that. This will help you both to bond and create a shared sense of humor.

– Know your audience: Make sure you understand the type of humor your partner or friends enjoy, and avoid humor that may be offensive to them.

– Be open to feedback: If you make a joke and it doesn't land well, be open to feedback from your partner or friends. It's important to understand what humor is and isn't appropriate in different situations.

– Take it in stride: If your partner or friends don't find your humor funny, don't take it personally. Everyone has different senses of humor, and it's okay if not everyone finds your jokes amusing.

Humor is an important aspect of relationships, both personal and professional. It can bring people closer together and help to reduce tension and stress in difficult situations. When it comes to relationships, laughter is often the best medicine.

One of the key benefits of humor in relationships is that it can help to create a sense of unity. When people share a good laugh together, they feel more connected to one another and are better able to bond. This is because humor creates an emotional connection, allowing people to feel seen and understood by one another.

Humor can also help to lighten the mood during difficult or stressful times. In a relationship, this can help to reduce tension and diffuse any negative emotions that may be present. When people can find a way to laugh together, even in difficult situations, they are better able to cope and move past any challenges that may arise.

Additionally, humor can also help to promote positive inter-actions. When people are laughing and having a good time, they are less likely to become defensive or upset. Instead, they are more likely to be open and responsive to one an-other, leading to more positive and productive interactions.

In the workplace, humor can also play a role in building strong relationships between colleagues. When coworkers can share a laugh and find humor in the workplace, they are able to build trust and camaraderie, leading to stronger teamwork and collaboration.

While humor can be a valuable tool in relationships, it is important to use it in a positive and healthy way. It is not al-ways appropriate to use humor to make fun of others or to diffuse a tense situation in a hurtful way. Instead, it is best to focus on using humor to bring people together and to cre-ate a positive and supportive environment.

When it comes to relationships, laughter truly is the best medicine. By incorporating humor into your interactions, you can create stronger bonds, reduce stress, and promote positive and productive interactions. Whether you are building relationships in your personal life or in the workplace, taking the time to share a good laugh can go a long way in creating and maintaining happy and fulfilling relationships.

33: Navigating Relationships in a Multicultural World

In a world that is becoming increasingly connected, it's not uncommon for people to form relationships with individuals from different cultures and backgrounds. Whether it's a romantic relationship, a friendship, or a professional connection, navigating these relationships can sometimes be challenging. However, with a little bit of understanding and patience, it's possible to build strong, fulfilling relationships that can last a lifetime.

One of the keys to success when it comes to multicultural relationships is open-mindedness. If you approach each interaction with a willingness to learn and understand the other person's perspective, you'll be well on your way to building a positive relationship. This means setting aside any preconceptions or biases you may have and being open to hearing the other person's experiences and beliefs.

Another important aspect of navigating multicultural relationships is communication. When people from different cultures come together, it's essential to have open, honest communication about each other's backgrounds, beliefs, and values. This can help to minimize misunderstandings and ensure that everyone feels heard and respected.

One important factor to consider in multicultural relationships is language. If you don't speak the same language as
the other person, it can be helpful to learn at least a few key
phrases in their native language. This shows that you're
making an effort to understand and connect with them, and
it can also help to break down any language barriers that
may exist.

It's also important to be mindful of cultural differences
when it comes to things like food, holidays, and social cus-
toms. For example, some cultures may place a strong em-
phasis on extended family and may expect a close relationship with in-laws, while others may value individual free-
dom and personal space more highly. Understanding these
cultural differences can help to ensure that everyone feels
comfortable and respected in the relationship.

Finally, it's important to remember that no two people are
exactly alike, regardless of their cultural background.
People are individuals, with their own unique experiences,
beliefs, and perspectives. By approaching each person with
respect and a willingness to learn, you can build strong, ful-

filling relationships with people from all over the world.

In conclusion, navigating relationships in a multicultural world requires a bit of effort, but it can also be incredibly rewarding. By being open-minded, communicating effectively, and understanding cultural differences, you can build relationships that are rich, meaningful, and long-lasting. So go ahead, reach out to someone from a different culture and start building a relationship today!

34: Building Strong Relationships: The Importance of Vulnerability

Introduction:

Vulnerability is an essential component of building strong relationships. Being vulnerable means being open, honest, and transparent about your feelings, thoughts, and experiences. In a world where everyone is striving for perfection and is constantly putting up a façade, vulnerability can be a challenging concept to grasp. However, the rewards of being vulnerable are immeasurable and can have a profound impact on the quality and longevity of your relationships.

What is Vulnerability?

Vulnerability is the quality of being exposed to the possibility of harm or damage. In the context of relationships, it refers to the act of opening up and revealing your true self to others. This means sharing your fears, insecurities, and emotions, even if they make you feel exposed or vulnerable. By doing so, you allow others to see the real you and connect with you on a deeper level.

34: BUILDING STRONG RELATIONSHIPS: THE IMPORTANCE OF VULNERABILITY

The Benefits of Vulnerability in Relationships:

– Closer Connections: By being vulnerable, you invite others to be vulnerable in return, leading to closer and more meaningful connections. When both partners are open and honest, they build trust, which is the foundation of any healthy relationship.

– Improved Communication: When you are vulnerable, you are more likely to communicate your thoughts and feelings effectively. This allows for open and honest conversations, which can lead to a deeper understanding of each other's needs and perspectives.

– Increased Emotional Intimacy: Vulnerability fosters emotional intimacy, which is crucial for the growth and stability of any relationship. Emotional intimacy refers to a deep emotional connection between two people, where both partners feel comfortable being their true selves.

– Decreased Jealousy and Envy: When you are vulnerable and open with your partner, they are more likely to do the same in return. This leads to a greater understanding of each other's experiences and emotions, which can decrease jealousy and envy.

– Increased Resilience: Relationships that are built on vulnerability are more resilient to stress and challenges. When partners have a strong emotional connection, they are better equipped to weather tough times and come out stronger on the other side.

Tips for Building Vulnerability in Relationships:

– Be Open and Honest: One of the most important steps in building vulnerability in relationships is being open and honest with your partner. Share your thoughts and feelings, even if they are difficult to express.

– Listen Without Judgment: When your partner is being vulnerable, it's important to listen without judgment. By creating a safe space for them to share their thoughts and feelings, you are building trust and fostering deeper connections.

– Practice Self-Reflection: In order to be vulnerable with others, you need to be vulnerable with yourself. This means being introspective and self-reflective, examining your own thoughts and emotions.

– Ask for What You Need: It's important to be clear about what you need from your partner, and to ask for it when necessary. When you express your needs openly and honestly, you build trust and increase the likelihood that your partner will respond positively.

– Be Vulnerable in Small Steps: If being vulnerable is challenging for you, start small. Share something personal with your partner, such as a fear or insecurity, and gradually build from there.

Conclusion:

Vulnerability is a powerful tool for building strong, meaningful relationships. By being open, honest, and transparent, you create a foundation of trust and emotional intimacy, which is essential for the growth and longevity of any relationship. Whether it's in your personal or professional life, making the effort to be vulnerable can lead to fulfilling connections, happier relationships, and a more fulfilling life.

35: The Power of Gratitude: Transforming Your Relationships

Gratitude is a powerful force that has the ability to transform relationships in a positive way. People who regularly express gratitude for the good things in their lives tend to have more fulfilling relationships, higher levels of happiness, and are generally more satisfied with their lives.

Gratitude has been shown to improve relationships in many ways. For example, expressing gratitude can help to strengthen emotional bonds, increase intimacy, and foster a sense of shared purpose between partners. It can also improve communication and help people to be more understanding and supportive of one another. Additionally, gratitude can help to foster a positive outlook, which can make it easier for people to find happiness in the present moment and appreciate what they have, rather than focusing on what they don't have.

One way to cultivate gratitude in relationships is by making it a habit to express gratitude regularly. This can be done by sharing with your partner or friend what you appreciate about them, or by taking the time to write down things that you are thankful for in a gratitude journal. Practicing gratitude can help to create a positive cycle, where one person's gratitude leads to the other person expressing gratitude, which then leads to more positive feelings and interactions.

Another way to cultivate gratitude in relationships is to actively look for things to be grateful for, rather than simply focusing on what's going wrong. For example, instead of focusing on the problems in your relationship, take the time to appreciate the small things that your partner does, such as making you a cup of tea or doing the dishes. By focusing on the positive aspects of your relationship, you will be more likely to build a strong, positive bond with your partner.

Gratitude can also be cultivated by practicing mindfulness, which is the practice of paying attention to the present moment without judgment. When you are mindful, you are able to fully appreciate the good things in your life, including the people you love. Practicing mindfulness can help you to be more present in your relationships, which can increase intimacy, reduce stress, and improve your overall sense of well-being.

In conclusion, cultivating gratitude in relationships is a

powerful way to transform relationships for the better. By expressing gratitude regularly, looking for things to be grateful for, and practicing mindfulness, you can build stronger, more fulfilling relationships and experience greater happiness and well-being. So, take the time to incorporate gratitude into your daily life, and watch as your relationships transform for the better.

36: Conclusion: The Future of Relationships and the Keys to Lasting Love and Fulfilling Connections

The conclusion of this book marks the end of our journey exploring the secrets to lasting love, fulfilling connections, and happy relationships. Throughout this guide, we have covered a wide range of topics, from managing relationships with friends and family to navigating relationships in a digital world, and from dealing with jealousy and envy to the importance of vulnerability and gratitude in building strong bonds.

At its core, this guide has been about empowering you to take control of your relationships and make them the best they can be. Whether you are looking to deepen existing relationships, build new ones, or heal from past heartache, this guide has provided you with the tools, tips, and insights you need to achieve your goals.

So what is the future of relationships? This is a question that only time will answer, but there are a few things we can be sure of. Firstly, the digital age will continue to impact the

36: CONCLUSION: THE FUTURE OF RELATIONSHIPS AND THE KEYS TO LASTING LOVE AND FULFILLING CONNECTIONS

way we interact with one another, and it is crucial that we find a way to balance our online and offline lives to foster meaningful connections. Secondly, as our world becomes increasingly diverse and multicultural, it is more important than ever to understand and respect one another's differences, and to learn how to navigate relationships in a multicultural world.

And finally, the future of relationships will be shaped by us. Each of us has the power to make a positive impact on the world through our relationships, and it is up to us to choose how we want to be remembered. Do we want to be known for our love, kindness, and compassion, or for our fear, anger, and hate? It is up to us to choose.

In conclusion, the keys to lasting love, fulfilling connections, and happy relationships are within our grasp. All we need to do is be open to the possibilities, be willing to put in the work, and have the courage to follow our hearts. So go out there, be brave, and build the relationships of your dreams!

Thank You

As we reach the end of this book, I want to say thanks for reading this book.

I want to get this information out to as many people as possible. If you found this book helpful, I would greatly appreciate you leaving me a review. This helps others find the book as well.

Disclaimer

This document is geared towards providing exact and reliable information in regards to the topic and issue covered. The publication is sold on the idea that the publisher is not required to render an accounting, officially permitted, or otherwise, qualified services. If advice is necessary, legal, financial, medical or professional, a practiced individual in the profession should be ordered.

This information is not presented by a financial or medical practitioner and is for entertainment, educational and informational purposes only. The content is not intended as a substitute for professional medical advice, diagnosis, or treatment. Always seek the advice of your physician or other qualified health care provider with any questions you may have regarding a medical condition. Never disregard professional medical advice or delay in seeking it because of something you have read.

The information provided herein is stated to be truthful and consistent, in that any liability, in terms of inattention or otherwise, by any usage or abuse of any policies, processes, or directions contained within is the solitary and utter responsibility of the recipient reader. Under no circumstances

DISCLAIMER

will any legal responsibility or blame be held against the
publisher for any reparation, damages, or monetary loss
due to the information herein, either directly or indirectly.

www.ingramcontent.com/pod-product-compliance
Lightning Source LLC
Chambersburg PA
CBHW060541130626
46553CB00002B/848